MY WORLD OF SCIENCE

Human Growth

Revised and Updated

Angela Royston

Heinemann Library
Chicago, Illinois

© 2003, 2008 Heinemann Library
a division of Pearson Inc.
Chicago, Illinois

Customer Service 888-454-2279
Visit our website at www.heinemannraintree.com

Designed by Joanna Hinton-Malivoire
Printed and bound in China by South China Printing Co. Ltd

12 11 10 09 08
10 9 8 7 6 5 4 3 2 1

New edition ISBN-13:   978-1-4329-1445-5 (hardcover)
                         978-1-4329-1467-7 (paperback)
         ISBN-10:   1-4329-1445-6 (hardcover)
                         1-4329-1467-7 (paperback)

The Library of Congress has cataloged the first edition as follows:
Royston, Angela
 Human Growth / Angela Royston
   p. cm – (My World of Science)
 Summary: Explains in simple text how the human body grows.
 Includes bibliographical references and index.
  ISBN 1-40340-989-7 (HC), 1-40343-196-5 (Pbk)
  1. Human growth-Juvenile literature.   [1. Growth.] I. Title.
 QP84 .R78 2003
 612.6'123-dc21

2002009400

CKC
j 612.6
c-1
5/14

Acknowledgements
The publishers would like to thank the following for permission to reproduce photographs: © Corbis pp. **9** (Jim Craigmyle), **25** (Envision); © Getty Images p. **22**; © Harcourt Education Ltd p. **11** (Tudor Photography); © Network/Jenny Matthews p. **21**; © Photodisc p. **7**; © Pictor International p. **23**; © Powerstock pp. **10**, **20**; © Robert Harding Picture Library p. **19**; © Science Photo Library pp. **16**, **18** (BSIP Chassenet), **28** (BSIP, LECA); © Trevor Clifford pp. **4**, **5**, **6**, **8**, **12**, **13**, **15**, **17**, **24**, **26**, **27**, **29**; unknown p. **14**.

Cover photograph reproduced with permission of © Getty Images (Stone/Sue Ann Miller).

The publishers would like to thank Jon Bliss for this assistance in the preparation of this book.

Every effort has been made to contact copyright holders of any material reproduced in this book. Any omissions will be rectified in subsequent printings if notice is given to the publishers.

Contents

Any words appearing in the text in bold, **like this**, are
explained in the glossary.

Growing Bigger

When you were born, you were a tiny baby. You grew bigger and heavier until you reached the size you are now.

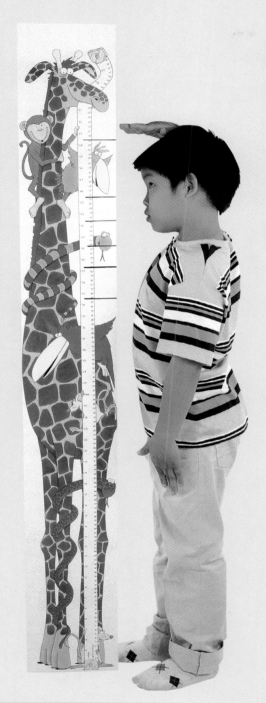

You will continue to grow all the time you are a child. Sometimes you will grow faster than others. When you stop growing, you will be a "grown up!"

Changing Size

Babies are different sizes when they are born. This baby is even smaller than the teddy bear. Most babies are around 20 inches long.

Babies and **toddlers** grow fast.
When they are three years old, most
children are more than half the
height of their **parents**.

Changing Weight

As well as growing taller, you become heavier. You probably weighed about 8 pounds when you were born. That is less than this bottle of water.

You weigh a lot more now. This girl is being weighed by a doctor. The doctor checks that she weighs about the right amount for her age.

Changing Shape

Your body changes shape as you grow. A baby's head is big compared to the rest of its body. Its arms and legs are short.

A **toddler**'s arms and legs grow faster than the rest of its body. When you are about six years old, your legs are nearly half your **height**.

How Tall Will You Grow?

Children grow at different rates. So some children are taller or smaller than other children. Which is the tallest child in this photo? (Answer on page 31.)

When you grow up you will probably be about the same **height** as your **parents**. If your parents are medium height, you probably will be, too.

Bones

Bones are hard and strong. They give your body its shape. Without bones, you would flop like jelly. Your bones grow longer and thicker as you grow.

skull

ribs

arm bones

spine

fingers

thigh bone

shin bone

toes

The bones in your **spine** allow you to twist and to bend forward and backward. Whose spine is bending forward the most? (Answer on page 31.)

Cells

Your body is made up of millions of different kinds of **cells**. Cells are so small that you need a special tool called a **microscope** to see them.

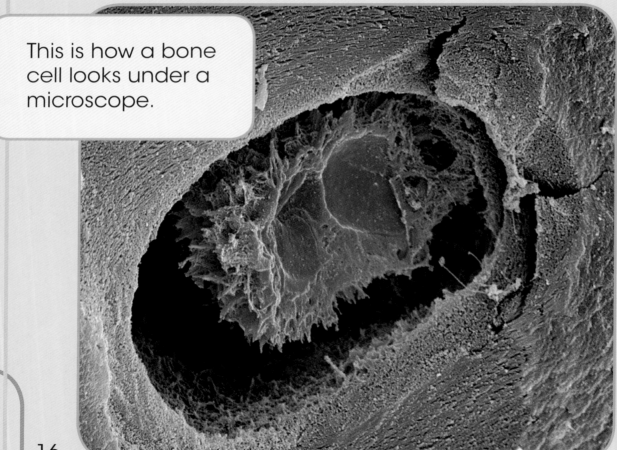

This is how a bone cell looks under a microscope.

Cells are like building blocks. Different parts of your body get bigger by adding on extra cells. Your body makes millions of new cells every day.

Two Sets of Teeth

When you were born, your first set of teeth was hidden in your **gums**. They slowly pushed through the gums. A second set formed behind them.

Your first set of teeth are called baby teeth. They begin to fall out when you are about six years old. The second set of teeth are bigger. You need to look after them so that they last the rest of your life.

Hair and Nails

Hair grows faster than most other parts of your body. Some people allow their hair to grow long. Others have it cut every few months.

Nails grow quickly, too. They grow from **cells** in the skin. This baby is having her nails cut to stop them from growing too long.

Healthy Food

You need to drink water and eat many kinds of food. These will help you to stay healthy and grow well. Different foods help your body in different ways.

Eating food with **protein** gives you the **energy** you need to play. Your body also needs protein to grow.

Food that Helps You to Grow

Meat, fish, and eggs contain a lot of **protein**. Cheese and beans contain lots of protein, too. You should eat some protein at every meal.

Bread, rice, and nuts also contain some protein. If you do not get enough protein, you will not grow very tall. Which of the foods below contain protein? (Answer on page 31.)

Food that Helps Your Bones

These foods all help your **bones** to grow long and strong. They contain **calcium**. Calcium in your bones makes them strong.

Calcium also makes your teeth stronger.
But you still need to clean your teeth
twice a day to keep them healthy.

Thinking and Learning

As children grow older, they begin to think and learn different things. This young child is learning to use his hands as he paints.

As you get older, you can do more difficult things. You also learn to read, to write, and to do math. Your **mind** never stops growing!

Glossary

bones hard parts of the body, underneath the skin and muscles

calcium something in food that makes your bones and teeth hard and strong

cells very small building blocks that make up the different parts of the body

energy power to move and to do things

gums flesh around the teeth

healthy being well and having all the parts of the body working properly

height how tall someone is

microscope tool that allows you to look at things that are normally too small to see

parents mother and father

protein something that the body needs to build new cells. It is found in some foods.

spine back bone

toddler child between about one and three years old

Answers

Page 12—The girl on the left is the tallest child.

Page 15—The spine of the girl on the right is bending forwards the most.

Page 25—The bread, peanut butter, and rice cakes all contain protein.

More Books to Read

Ganeri, Anita. *How Living Things Grow*. Chicago: Heinemann Library, 2006.

Royston, Angela. *My Amazing Body: Staying Healthy*. Chicago: Raintree, 2004.

Thomas, Pat. *My Amazing Body: A First Look at Health and Fitness*. New York: Barron's Educational Series, 2002.

Index